EXTREME
COLOURING
Tattoos

CARLTON
BOOKS

Ready for an extraordinary challenge? Try these tattoos! The designs in the following pages are either inspired by tattoos or the inspiration for them. Some are remarkably complex. And if you think that no artist could tattoo such designs, think again.

Mehndi, the temporary tattoos popular in Asia, Africa, and the Middle East, are often remarkable for their delicacy. Skilled mehndi artists are much in demand and able to command high fees. Mehndi tattoos fade, of course. Any other type of tattoo is permanent and will follow you through life. Skilled artists will remind you of this, and will tell you to carefully consider your choice of design.

There are, of course, recurring motifs, and as you color your way across these pages, you'll learn some of the meanings often attached to them. From lions to eagles and roses to wings, tattoos make it possible to express an aspect of your character or what you believe. Combine several images and you'll combine several ideas, which helps to make the tattoo unique to you. In these pages are designs combining roses with dragons, for example, or skulls with flowers.

Today, people of all ages and all backgrounds are getting themselves inked. That's not always been the case, and tattoos have often been associated with particular types of individuals. Swallows have long been popular with sailors. Koi carp are a traditional badge of honor for criminals in Japan. Mehndi's temporary designs are traditional for brides.

So, gather your pens, crayons, even highlighters and see if you can match the best artists in the business.

MEHNDI

Mehndi is a traditional form of temporary tattoo and is particularly associated with wedding ceremonies and brides. The intricate designs, for both hands and feet, are created using henna paste, which stains the skin orange. The color oxidizes and darkens over time to a reddish brown that will last for up to three weeks. Indian designs tend to be complex, often incorporating patterns within patterns. Flowers and peacocks are popular.

OWLS

The owl carries powerful meanings. It is a bird of prey that hunts silently by night, which means that some cultures associate it with death. This is not necessarily to be feared: the owl may protect us from danger, or the "death" may simply mark a transition in life. The bird's famously sharp eyesight means that it is also linked with knowledge, wisdom, and experience.

GECKO LIZARDS

The word *tattoo* is derived from *ta-tau* or *ta-tu*, used by Polynesian peoples. Before the English adopted this word, the art form was known in the Western world as scarring or staining. Polynesian tattoos are distinctive for their thick black shapes, much like the geckos on the right here. Geckos have an important role in the various Polynesian cultures. Their ability to regrow their tails makes them a symbol of regrowth. And featuring geckos in a design will bring good fortune.

DRAGONS

Across Asia, dragons are revered and carry powerful meanings. Creating fire, flying through the air, and living underground, they have mastered nature. Linked to the sun, they embody power and frighten their enemies. Their mythical status associates them with magic and the possibility of locating our inner power. They are also thought to bring good fortune. It's no surprise, then, that dragons are an ever-popular design.

SKULL WITH FLOWERS

Get a tattoo, and the design will be with you until you die. This partly explains why death themes have long been a popular choice, suggesting an acceptance of one's own mortality. Adding flowers to the design creates a powerful contrast, reminding us of the struggle between life and death, beauty and decay. This means the design is sometimes chosen to mark a turning point in one's life.

LOVE BIRDS

Perhaps inevitably, love birds are a symbol of undying love
and commitment. They represent the joy of a relationship
and the security it brings. Designs are often brightly colored,
while a pattern that uses only black may reflect the loss of a partner
who has died. For all the romance implied, artists often advise
clients to avoid adding the name of a loved one. Tattoos are for life;
relationships might not be.

HENNA FLOWERS

The mehndi ceremony, when prospective brides are decorated with temporary tattoos, is one of the world's oldest wedding traditions. Flowers are an ever-popular design, and not just for obvious reasons. They will suit whatever the bride is wearing. The designs cover both hands, often mirror images of each other, an effect that is particularly striking when the bride holds both hands together.

DOLPHINS

A dolphin tattoo makes a positive statement. Cultures across the world have embraced these intelligent animals. Playful and intelligent, they have a strong sense of community, and stories of dolphins saving sailors from drowning are common. With no boundaries to limit them, dolphins are seen as free spirits riding wherever the waves take them. As a result, dolphin tattoos are popular within the surfing community.

TIGER, DRAGON, AND SKULLS

The skull can take on different meanings. Here, alongside a dragon and tiger, it represents power. The tiger and dragon are powerful creatures, and Chinese folklore tells us that the two are mortal enemies. The dragon is a wise creature; the tiger is an animal of brute strength. The struggle between the two is the struggle between mind and body, striving to achieve balance.

CHINESE DRAGON

The shape of the dragon means it suits being located on various parts of the body: on the shoulder, winding across the torso, or down the length of an arm. Dragons are an increasingly popular tattoo design, in part because they are easy to customize. Do you want your dragon to breathe fire? Are its wings open for flight? Do you want multiple colors, or color for only its eyes?

SKULL WITH FLOWERS

A skull with flowers is a design that takes its cue from Mexico's Day of the Dead, or Día de Muertos. Marigolds have a particular importance, for their scent is believed to wake the souls of the dead and guide them back to the world of the living. The festival is a celebration of those who have died, and a tattoo of a skull is likely to be done in honor of a particular individual.

EYE OF PROVIDENCE

The all-seeing eye of God is an idea that has long existed in many cultures, but the Eye of Providence developed specifically from Christianity. The triangle enclosing the eye is a reference to the Holy Trinity: the Father, the Son, and the Holy Spirit. The wings framing the design suggest that God is not merely seeing everything, but is also watching over us and protecting us via guardian angels.

WOLF

The dream catcher below and the crescent moon above indicate
that this is the wolf of Native American culture. As such, the wolf
is a symbol of power and wisdom, and is an animal that acts as our
guardian. Indeed, for the Shoshone people, the wolf was the creator.
For the Quileute, wolves were transformed into the first humans.
For the Anishinaabe, the wolf is a loyal friend.

PEGASUS

Pegasus, the winged horse of Greek mythology, can carry different meanings. Flying freely across the skies, he is a free spirit. He can also carry inspiration to us from the muses, an idea that links him to the imagination. Pegasus also carried Bellerephon, the warrior who destroyed the monstrous Chimera. Together they became the insignia for British airborne forces during World War II, and for Italian partisans resisting the Nazi occupation.

EAGLE

Across cultures, the eagle has long been a symbol of power. Since
Roman times, it has been associated with the idea of victory. Over
the centuries, its symbolism has developed to include the ideas
of righteous authority and justice. It is a patriotic choice not just
for Americans—you'll find eagles on the coats of arms of countries
across the globe, from Poland to Panama, Iceland to Indonesia.

SEAHORSES

They may not be a particularly common tattoo design, but seahorses carry interesting meanings. It is the male who carries the fertilized eggs and waits for them to hatch, so the seahorse has become a symbol of fatherhood and protection. Traditionally, too, the seahorse is said to guard the souls of those who die at sea, so for sailors it is a sign of good luck.

BULL

The bull represents power and strength. An angry bull, as here,
often implies masculine energy, though its overriding meaning
is opposition. This is the tattoo of choice for those who pride
themselves on never backing down. Yet there is another aspect to
the bull. With its power harnessed by farmers across the centuries,
the bull has also become a symbol of cooperation.

BUTTERFLIES

Butterflies are said to represent freedom, making them a good choice for self-confessed free spirits. That said, is this now a cliché? It's a question tattoo artists might ask. They've likely been in the business for years, if not decades, so when an artist asks you to reconsider, it may be worth listening. They'll have seen fashions come and go, and know of clients who admit their regrets in choosing a butterfly design.

ANGEL

Across the world, angels are traditionally messengers between ourselves and higher powers. So an angel tattoo is often a direct expression of faith. Equally strong is the idea of the angel as protector, which implies both strength and love. This is a tattoo to suggest confidence in the future, and the belief that obstacles can be overcome. These associations may explain why angel tattoos are becoming increasingly popular.

WOLF

The wolf is a good choice for those who like to consider themselves as warriors, able to go it alone. A tattoo artist can enhance this meaning by placing it above a major muscle group. A twitch of the muscles can make the wolf seem even more threatening. Yet the wolf offers more positive meanings too. Wolf packs stick together, so the wolf is also a symbol of loyalty.

ORCHIDS

Their sheer beauty means that orchids are popular tattoos, while
their elegance means that large designs are often attractive. Since
black is the only color of orchid not seen in nature, expect these
tattoos to be colorful. Pink is for happiness; red for passion; yellow
for new beginnings. Note the spots on the petals. These are said
to represent the blood of Christ, making orchids a good choice to
express one's faith.

KOI CARP

Koi carp are traditional symbols of family, so you can use different colors within a tattoo to represent different family members. Red is for a mother and the intense love she gives her family. Black suggests a strong father. At the same time, red koi embody courage and power, while black koi imply success. Tattooing these koi onto your skin is a way to draw these attributes to you.

HENNA

This design suggests Arabic influences. While Indian designs avoid leaving skin untouched, Arabic designs are more free-flowing and often incorporate bare patches. Like all henna tattoos, any effects will be temporary, but it's worth remembering that henna itself is a natural sunblock. This means that a design exposed to sunlight will leave pale lines after the henna has faded, lasting as long as your tan does. Remember, though, you still need to apply sunscreen.

FLOWERS

It's easy in the West to assume that flower tattoos are more appropriate for women. There's no such prejudice in Asia. In Japan, cherry blossoms evoke the transience of life, while an orchid suggests bravery. To the Chinese, the orchid represents integrity, while the chrysanthemum symbolizes happiness, attracts good luck, and carries the promise of a long life. The lotus changes meaning with its color: white and pink imply purity and devotion, while red, purple, and blue imply knowledge, wisdom, or rebirth.

ORNATE FLOWERS

Part of the appeal of tattoos is that they can hide secrets in plain sight. This abstract design based on flowers seems innocent enough, but it may imply defiance. Its style echoes the traditional folk art of Ukraine, particularly the traditional designs used to decorate Easter eggs (*pysanky*). These were banned by the Soviets, and such traditional folk art was revived only when Ukraine regained independence.

MEDUSA

With eyes that could turn a man to stone and snakes writhing
around her head, Medusa was a powerful woman. As a tattoo,
she offers you protection from those who would harm you. Greek
mythology describes her death at the hands of Perseus, who cut off
her head. Out of her body sprang a winged horse, Pegasus, and from
this comes the idea that Medusa can also represent transformation.

ANGEL WINGS

Angel wings can carry multiple meanings, all of them positive. They may simply be a symbol of protection, the wings suggesting the presence of a guardian angel. They may be a reminder of a loved one, now passed and in heaven. They may also have religious significance. Wings obviously imply flight, which is easily associated with the idea of freedom. They also suggest the ability to rise above obstacles.

EGYPT HORUS FALCON

Horus, the sky god of Ancient Egypt, took the form of a falcon to fly across the sky. From this vantage point, he could see everything, so the falcon has become a symbol of both knowledge and power. The falcon also suggests determination and commitment. It is a patient predator, circling high in the air and watching carefully before swooping down to catch its prey.

SCARAB BEETLE

For the people of Ancient Egypt, the scarab beetle pushed its dung ball across the sands in the same way that the sun moves across the sky. They also noticed that a young scarab beetle emerges fully formed from the ball in which its egg was laid. These two ideas combined to associate the scarab with the divine world and to make it a symbol of regeneration.

PHOENIX

The mythical phoenix offers a powerful promise of hope and renewal. Every time it is destroyed by fire, it emerges stronger from the ashes. Such symbolism offers great opportunities for designing a tattoo. Expect strong, vibrant colors, especially for its fiery tail feathers. And remember, this is a mythical creature, so it will look exactly how you want it to. No wonder it's popular around the world.

LION

The lion is the king of the jungle, so this tattoo is the ultimate symbol of power. A lion's head, rather than a full body, is the most common design, and artists say they most often locate it on the shoulder. They add that a lion's head is a good design for covering scars after accidents or surgery. Given that the lion is associated with survival, this seems appropriate.

KOI CARP

Koi carp are a common design for the traditional Japanese form of tattooing known as Irezumi. They are particularly associated with criminals, and indeed are a badge of honor, because these fish are a symbol of bravery and their images may only be worn by those who have shown no fear. Since koi carp must swim upstream, they also represent perseverance and strength of character.

DREAM CATCHER AND OWL

The dream catcher, which originated among the Ojibwe people, is said to protect you as you sleep. Capturing bad dreams within its web, it allows only good dreams to reach you. Owls too are dream catchers, believed to bring messages to us from beyond the world of our senses. Combining the two in one image is said to offer strong protection and ensure good comes into your life.

SERPENT

Snakes carry multiple meanings, both positive and negative. Their venom makes them creatures to be wary of, but this association is not necessarily negative. Venom can also be used to protect. Wearing a snake tattoo is also a warning to others: "Don't trample on me." Remember, too, that snakes regularly shed their skin. Literally leaving their past behind, they are a powerful symbol of transformation and renewal.

BIRD OF PREY

A bird of prey alongside an inverted triangle and crescent moons
means this design is particularly suitable for a woman. Why? Birds
of prey are known for their sharpness of vision, which means they
become symbols of intelligence. An inverted triangle is a symbol of
feminine energy, while the moon is often associated with feminine
power. Taken together, they suggest that this design celebrates a
woman's strength and intuition.

SWALLOWS

Traditionally, swallows are popular with sailors. Why? Swallows are often the first birds to be seen when approaching land, so they carry the promise of a safe return. For every 5,000 nautical miles sailed, a sailor is allowed to add one swallow tattoo. The more tattoos, the luckier the sailor. And if fate brings only death at sea, the swallow will carry the soul to heaven.

HENNA FLOWER BUDS

We have been using henna for tattoos for thousands of years. Similarly, the flower buds in this design have a long tradition. They symbolize the new life a bride is embarking on and promise that love will flourish. The delicate outlines of the tattoo do require a steady hand. Much like permanent tattoos, there is little room for mistakes. Henna, though, does fade . . .

ORCHIDS

Orchids are found across the world, and have developed a variety of meanings. In China, they are a symbol of what is precious and rare; elsewhere, they are considered an aphrodisiac. For women, an orchid tattoo reflects their beauty; for men, it represents strength. Since there are almost 28,000 species of orchid, almost any color is appropriate for tattoos, from soft pastels to vibrant purples and pinks.

BUTTERFLY ON A FINGER

The most remarkable transformation in nature is probably that of the caterpillar to the butterfly. So, when a butterfly lands on you, the belief is that this represents significant change for you. The change is likely to be remarkable, but the promise is that you can handle it with the grace of a butterfly in flight. That said, who needs symbolism when butterflies make such beautiful and colorful tattoos?

MANDALA

Mandalas are often regarded as a form of flower tattoo. That the flower shape tends to be abstract rather than obvious means these designs are also popular with men. The advantage of mandalas is that they are equally effective at any size. Large designs suit thighs or even the rib cage, while simple, small designs enhance wrists. Most mandalas are often simply monochrome, but accent colors work well too.

FLOWERS

Flowers often make the most beautiful tattoos. Using only blacks and grays can create subtle effects, but flowers are an opportunity for skilled artists to display their use of color. Designs may feature soft pastels as delicate as watercolors or the vivid contrasts of jewel-bright colors. Alternatively, artists may prefer to use only one color, such as red, to contrast with the black outlines.

MASKS

These masquerade masks take their cue from the masks worn during the Carnival of Venice. Covering only the eyes and not the full face, they lend mystery but not full anonymity. It is said they were first worn by an actress who did not want to disguise her beauty. Perhaps because of their lacey elements, masquerade masks are popular designs for women wanting tattoos.

LION

A tattoo of a roaring lion sends a message that is both powerful and flexible. *Powerful* because it says you are to be respected, even feared. After all, a roaring lion is preparing for a fight. *Flexible* because it can take on different meanings throughout your life. The person you were in your twenties, raring to go, may mellow into someone fiercely protective of their children and grandchildren.

ROSES

Roses are an ever-popular tattoo. They are most commonly associated with love and beauty, but their color is also significant. Red obviously symbolizes romance, but may also represent sacrifice. Pink suggests first love and innocence. Blue stands for the impossible, white for purity, and black for remembrance. The beauty of the rose is a contrast to their thorns, which remind us of the sacrifices required of love.

BABOON

Baboons live in large troops, so a tattoo is the mark of a good team player. A design of a yawning baboon represents power, since males will yawn to show off their teeth as a warning before a fight. Baboons are also associated with wisdom. This reflects their status in traditional African cultures, which consider them the most intelligent of animals.

MANDALA

Mandala is the Sanskrit word for *circle*, and these designs are based around a circle. This shape represents balance and wholeness, extending outward beyond itself and reaching inward to the center. That's a good reminder of how we ourselves should act. What's more, neither the beginning of a circle nor its end is visible, so a mandala tattoo represents the idea that life itself is never-ending.

DRAGON AND ROSES

Tattoos often combine dragons with flowers to offer meanings
unique to the wearer. Chinese dragons are often associated with
good luck. Note too their claws, which symbolize fearlessness
and the ability to conquer evil. Beside them are roses, a symbol
of prosperity. Fully open, they are also a promise of creativity.
So, which color will you choose? Yellow for happiness, orange for
energy, or red for passion?

THIS IS A CARLTON BOOK

Published by Carlton Books Ltd
20 Mortimer Street
London W1T 3JW

Copyright © 2016 Carlton Books Ltd

A CIP catalogue record for this book is available from the British Library

1 2 3 4 5 6 7 8 9 10

ISBN 978-1-78097-896-3

Printed in China

All illustrations created from images supplied courtesy of Shutterstock.com